Big
WORDS
FOR Little Paleontologists

The Dino Dictionary Every Little Explorer Needs

Lisa M. Gerry

Hi! I'm a Ceratogaulus (sir-AT-oh-GALL-us), a prehistoric horned gopher. You can call me Atto. I'll be your guide. Let's go!

NATIONAL GEOGRAPHIC
WASHINGTON, D.C.

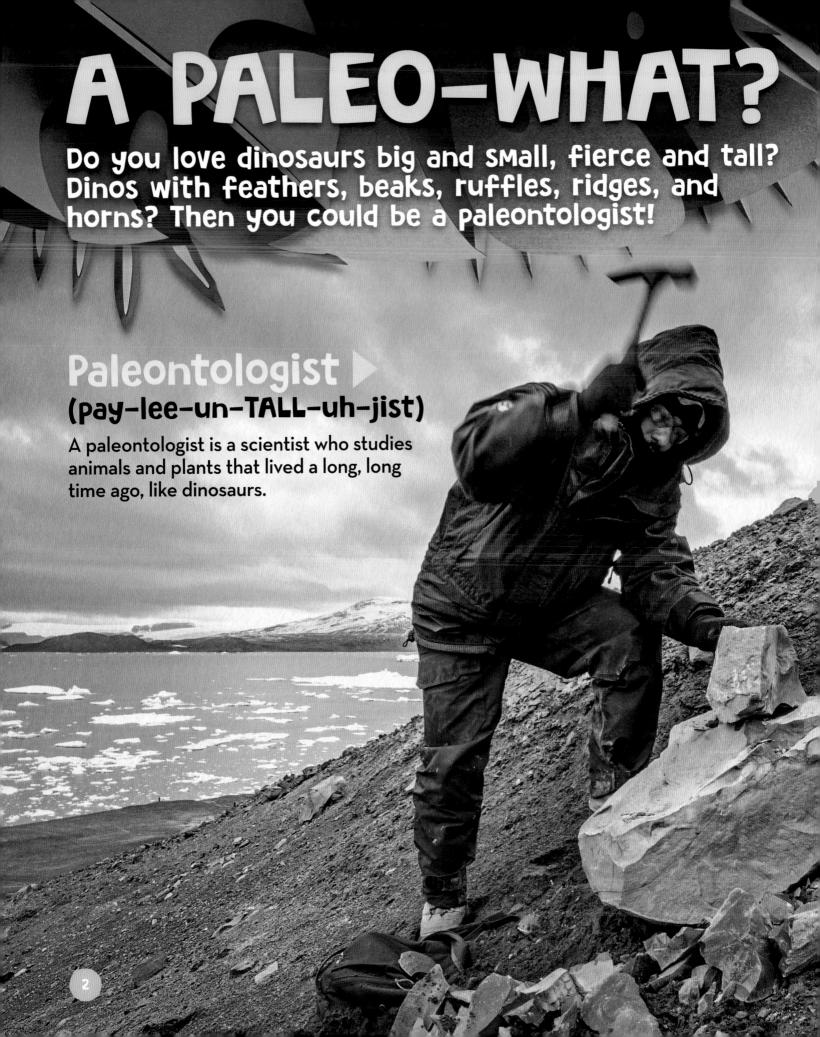

A PALEO-WHAT?

Do you love dinosaurs big and small, fierce and tall? Dinos with feathers, beaks, ruffles, ridges, and horns? Then you could be a paleontologist!

Paleontologist ▶
(pay-lee-un-TALL-uh-jist)

A paleontologist is a scientist who studies animals and plants that lived a long, long time ago, like dinosaurs.

Fossil (FA-sul) ▶

A fossil is a preserved part or trace of an ancient animal or plant that lived at least 10,000 years ago. Paleontologists find fossils buried in the earth. Most of these fossils are bones or teeth.

◀ Excavate (EK-skuh-VAYT)

To excavate a fossil means to take it out of the ground. Paleontologists have to be very careful not to break the fossils they dig up.

Atto Says!

Shells, leaves, and even footprints can be preserved, or saved, as fossils in rocks.

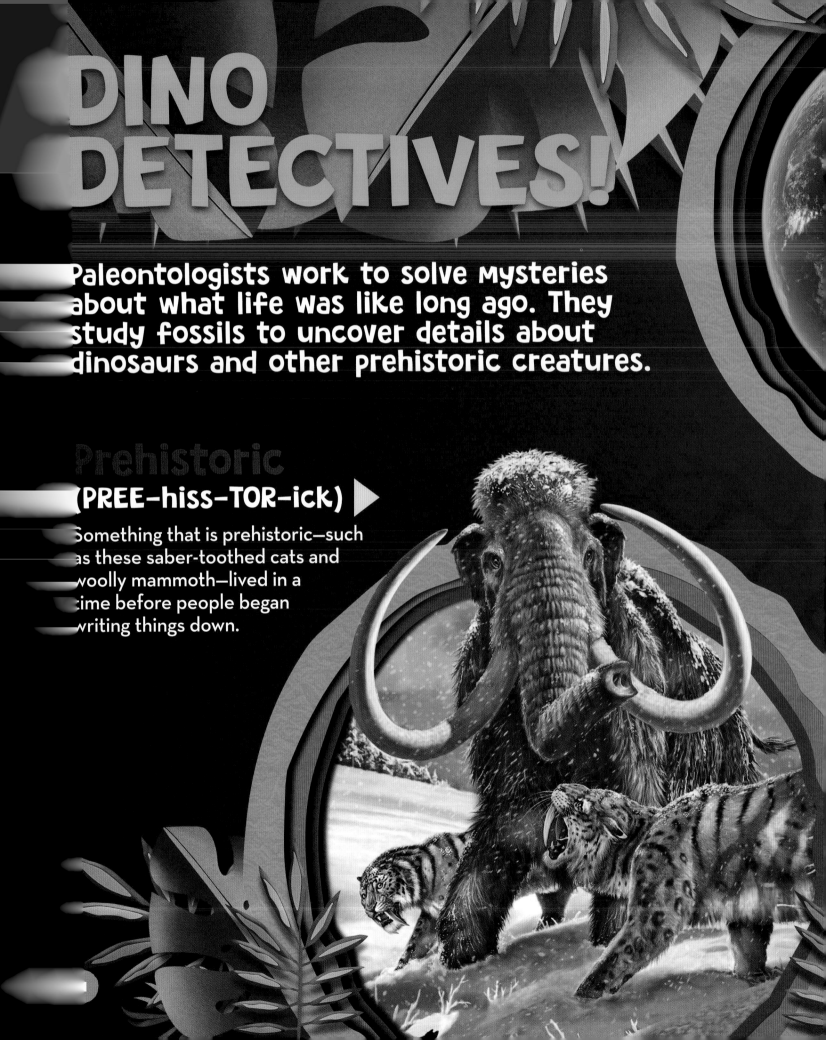

DINO DETECTIVES!

Paleontologists work to solve mysteries about what life was like long ago. They study fossils to uncover details about dinosaurs and other prehistoric creatures.

Prehistoric

(PREE-hiss-TOR-ick) ▶

Something that is prehistoric—such as these saber-toothed cats and woolly mammoth—lived in a time before people began writing things down.

Mesozoic Era
(meh–suh–ZOH–ick EH–ruh)

Dinosaurs lived on Earth during the Mesozoic Era, a time period that began about 250 MILLION years ago. That's *waaayyyyy* before humans lived on Earth.

Extinct ▶
(ek–STINKT)

When something is extinct, there's no more of it left alive on Earth. Most dinosaurs became extinct millions of years ago, after a huge meteorite hit the planet.

Atto Says!

A meteorite is a rock from outer space!

GRAB YOUR TOOLS!

Sometimes dino bones and other fossils are inside stone that is super hard. You need special tools to get the fossils out!

Chisel (CHIH-zul)

A chisel has a sharp metal edge. It is used to break away the rock around a fossil. First you place the blade of the chisel on the rock. Then you hit the top of the chisel with a hammer.

▼

Trowel (TROW-ul)

A trowel is flat and made of metal. Paleontologists use a trowel to move loose rock or dirt or to scoop up soft soil or mud.

▲

AWL (ALL)

This small, pointy tool is used to *scrape, scrape, scrape* away at fossils while they are still trapped in rock.

◀

Brush (BRUSH) ▶

When paleontologists get close to a fossil, they use a brush to wipe away the dust and bits of rock.

Atto Says!

Sometimes paleontologists find a full skeleton. Other times a fossil find is just one bone or tooth.

FANTASTIC FOSSILS!

Fossils come in all shapes and sizes. They can be found in deserts, mountains, and even at the beach.

Micropaleontology

(MY-croh-pay-lee-un-TALL-uh-jee)

Micropaleontology is the study of the teeniest, tiniest fossils, like these pollen fossils. These fossils are so small you need a powerful microscope to see them.

Paleobotany
(PAY-lee-oh-BOT-uh-nee)

Paleobotany is the study of prehistoric plants. To find out what kinds of trees and plants were around before humans lived, paleobotanists look for plant fossils.

Trilobites
(TRY-loh-bites)

Trilobites lived more than 500 million years ago. Scientists think these small animals moved along the ocean floor and ate algae—and sometimes other trilobites!

Coprolites
(KAH-pruh-lites)

Coprolites are fossilized poop!

Atto Says!

Paleontologists can figure out what dinosaurs ate by studying coprolites.

MEET THE MEAT-EATERS!

When carnivores (KAR-nih-vors) got hungry, there's only one thing these dinos wanted to eat: other animals.

Tyrannosaurus rex
(tie-RAN-oh-SORE-us rex)

Tyrannosaurus rex, nicknamed T. rex, was a fierce hunter. Its teeth were as long as bananas!

MORE CARNIVORES

Spinosaurus ▶
(SPINE–oh–SORE–us)

Spinosaurus had a long jaw, like a crocodile. It is the biggest carnivorous dinosaur paleontologists have ever found!

Atto Says!

Carnivores had long, sharp teeth—perfect for tearing meat. Check out this tyrannosaur tooth!

◀ **Sinosauropteryx**
(SINE-oh-SORE-op-TARE-icks)

Sinosauropteryx fossils helped paleontologists discover that some dinosaurs had feathers.

▲

Velociraptor
(vel-OSS-ih-RAP-tore)

This birdlike dinosaur ran on its back legs and was covered in feathers. It used the long claw on each of its feet to pin down its prey.

HELLO, HERBIVORES!

No meat for herbivores (UR-bih-vors).
These dinosaurs were plant-eaters.

Kosmoceratops
(COZ-moh-SERR-uh-tops)

Kosmoceratops had a lot of horns and
spikes decorating its face. It had one horn
on the tip of its nose, one on each cheek, and
one above each eye, and then 10 spikes at the

Ankylosaurus
(AN–kee–loh–SORE–us)

Ankylosaurus was covered in spikes and hard plates made of bone. It could swing around its big tail like a club.

MORE HERBIVORES

Psittacosaurus
(SIT-ah-coh-SORE-us)

Psittacosaurus had a hard beak that it used to cut through plants. Then it used the teeth in the back of its jaws to chew up the plants.

Giraffatitan
(jih-RAF-ah-TIE-tan)

This big dino's superlong neck helped it reach tasty leaves at the top of trees.

Atto Says!

The biggest dinosaurs ever were herbivores. They needed to eat hundreds of pounds of food every day!

Tsintaosaurus
(sin-tau-SORE-us)

Tsintaosaurus had a toothless beak and a long bone that grew from its forehead. It's been nicknamed the "duckfaced unicorn."

OH MY, OMNIVORES!

Omnivores (AHM-nih-vors) mixed it up at mealtime. These dinos ate both meat and plants!

Ornithomimus ▶

(or-NITH-oh-MY-mus)

Ornithomimus looked a bit like an ostrich. It was covered in feathers. It also had a long neck and a beak.

◀ Deinocheirus

(DINE-oh-KYE-rus)

Deinocheirus had a big sail, or hump, on its back. It also had long arms, and huge claws on its hands.

Gigantoraptor
(jie-GAN-toe-RAP-tore)

Gigantoraptor was a huge birdlike dinosaur. Scientists think it was one of the largest dinosaurs with a beak.

Dromiceiomimus
(droh-MEE-see-oh-MY-mus)

Dromiceiomimus might have been the fastest dinosaur. Scientists think it could run as fast as a lion!

WELCOME, WINGED WONDERS!

Paleontologists think that some winged dinosaurs and other prehistoric creatures could fly like birds, and that others just glided through the air like kites.

Microraptor ▶

(MY-croh-RAP-tore)

This little dino was about the size of a crow. It did not fly, but it could glide from branch to branch. Scientists think it may have used the feathers on its tail to steer.

Scansoriopteryx

(SCAN-sore-ee-OP-tare-icks)

This small creature had feathers and could glide through the air. It used its strong, sharp claws to climb trees. ▼

Ambopteryx
(am–BOH–tare–icks)

Ambopteryx used its batlike wings to glide through the air, like flying squirrels today. Scientists think this small, fuzzy dinosaur also had long tail feathers.

▶

◀ ## Archaeopteryx
(ARK–ee–OP–tare–icks)

Paleontologists think *Archaeopteryx* could use its wings to fly. It was about the size of a small chicken.

Pterosaurs ▶
(TER–uh–sores)

Pterosaurs were a group of flying reptiles that lived at the same time as dinosaurs. Scientists think they used their wings for flying as well as walking.

Sharovipteryx
(shar–oh–VIP–tare–icks)

Sharovipteryx was a lizard-like reptile that lived at the same time as the very earliest dinosaurs. Its wings were on its back legs! ▼

UNDER THE SEA

Paleontologists know that prehistoric creatures like these once roamed the seas. How do they know? From discovering their fossils, of course!

Ammonites
(AM-moh-nites)

Ammonites were squidlike animals that had spiral-shaped shells. Their fossils are found all around the world.

▼

Tusoteuthis
(TOO-soh-TOO-this)

Tusoteuthis was a kind of giant squid. It had long tentacles and could grow to be the length of a school bus.

▲

▲

Plesiosaurus
(please–EE–oh–SORE–us)
This prehistoric reptile had a large flat body, fins, a short tail, and a very long neck. Paleontologists think it swung its neck from side to side to catch fish.

MORE SPECTACULAR SWIMMERS

Megalodon ▶
(MEH-guh-luh-don)

Megalodon is thought to be the largest shark that ever lived. Its teeth could be as long as pencils! It ate dolphins, whales, and other sea creatures.

Thalattoarchon
(thuh-LOT-oh-AR-con)

Thalattoarchon was a reptile with a snout like a dolphin and lots of pointy teeth—perfect for grabbing on to slippery snacks like fish and squid.

Basilosaurus ▶
(bah-SILL-oh-SORE-us)

Basilosaurus was one of Earth's first whales. It could grow to be as long as a trailer truck.

PRESENTING PREHISTORIC MAMMALS!

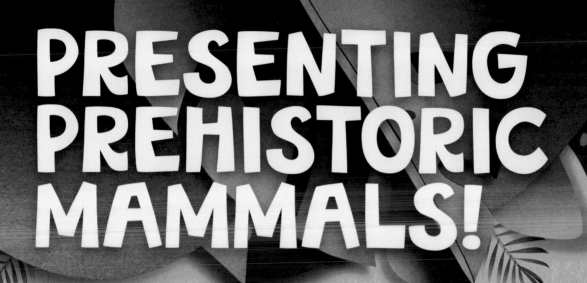

Millions of years ago, all sorts of creatures lived on Earth, including mammals. How do we know? Fossils, fossils, fossils!

Glyptodon ▶
(GLIP-toe-don)

Glyptodon had a very hard shell that protected it from hungry animals. It was the size of a small car!

Atto Says! Mammals are a group of animals that includes dogs, bears, and kangaroos. I'm a mammal, and so are you!

Tinimomys
(tie-nee-MOH-mees)
This itty-bitty mammal weighed about as much as one slice of bread. It was so tiny, it could have fit on the tip of your nose.

Elasmotherium
(ee-LAZ-moh-THEER-ee-um)
Elasmotherium had a huge horn on its face. It is an ancient relative of the modern-day rhinoceros.

MORE BIG WORDS

Argentinosaurus
(ahr-gen-TEEN-oh-SORE-us)

Argentinosaurus may have been the heaviest dinosaur. It weighed about the same as 20 elephants! *(See front cover.)*

Compsognathus
(KOMP-sog-NAH-thus)

This small dinosaur was about the size of a turkey. It ran fast on its two back legs to catch lizards, insects, and other small animals.

Huayangosaurus ▶
(hwah-YANG-oh-SORE-us)

Huayangosaurus had a row of spikes all along its back and at the tip of its tail to keep predators away.

◀ Invertebrate Fossils
(in-VER-tuh-bret FA-suls)

Invertebrate fossils are from animals without backbones, such as trilobites, ammonites, shellfish, and snails.

Longisquama
(long-ih-SKWAH-muh)

This prehistoric reptile lived in the forest. It had long club-shaped growths sticking out of its back.

Mapusaurus
(MAP-oo-SORE-us)

Mapusaurus hunted in packs. These dinosaurs could take down other dinos 10 times their size! *(See front cover.)*

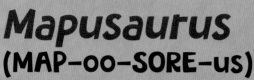

Micropachycephalosaurus
(MY-croh-PACK-ee-SEF-ah-loh-SORE-us)

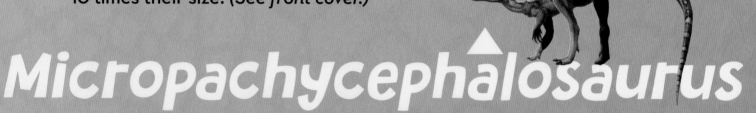

This dinosaur was one of the smallest dinos, but it has the longest name of them all! It walked on its hind legs and ate plants.

Quetzalcoatlus
(KET-sal-koh-AHT-lus)

Quetzalcoatlus was about as tall as a giraffe. It was one of the largest flying animals to ever live on Earth.

Atto Says!

Looking for a challenge? Let's see if you can master these tongue twisters!

Therizinosaurus
(THERE-ih-ZIN-oh-SORE-us)

This giant dinosaur had huge claws. Scientists think it may have used its claws to dig up bugs to eat.

Vertebrate Fossils
(VER-tuh-bret FA-suls)

Vertebrate fossils are from animals with backbones. These include birds, mammals, and dinosaurs and other reptiles.

For Abigail, Andy,
and Jackson, who teach me new
big words all the time! —L.M.G.

NATIONAL GEOGRAPHIC and Yellow Border Design are trademarks of the National Geographic Society, used under license.

Since 1888, the National Geographic Society has funded more than 14,000 research, conservation, education, and storytelling projects around the world. National Geographic Partners distributes a portion of the funds it receives from your purchase to National Geographic Society to support programs including the conservation of animals and their habitats. To learn more, visit natgeo.com/info.

For more information, visit nationalgeographic.com, call 1-877-873-6846, or write to the following address:

National Geographic Partners, LLC
1145 17th Street NW
Washington, DC 20036-4688 U.S.A.

For librarians and teachers: nationalgeographic.com/books/librarians-and-educators

More for kids from National Geographic: natgeokids.com

National Geographic Kids magazine inspires children to explore their world with fun yet educational articles on animals, science, nature, and more. Using fresh storytelling and amazing photography, *Nat Geo Kids* shows kids ages 6 to 14 the fascinating truth about the world—and why they should care. **natgeo.com/subscribe**

For rights or permissions inquiries, please contact National Geographic Books Subsidiary Rights: bookrights@natgeo.com

Designed by Brett Challos

The publisher would like to thank the following people for making this book possible: Nizar Ibrahim, paleontologist and National Geographic Explorer, for his expert review of the book; Franco Tempesta, illustrator; and Katherine Kling, fact-checker. Special thanks to paper artist Maren Schabhüser for creating Atto the prehistoric horned gopher. Thanks also to Lori Epstein, photo manager; Emily Fego, project editor; and Lauren Sciortino and David Marvin, design associates.

All dinosaur artwork by Franco Tempesta/ © National Geographic Partners, LLC, unless otherwise noted below. All cut paper artwork of horned gopher and leaves by Maren Schabhüser/ Mendola Ltd. Background throughout (reptile skin), cla78/ Shutterstock.

Cover (*Mapusaurus*), © Franco Tempesta; (pterosaurs), © Franco Tempesta; front flap (speech bubble), Roman Yaroshchuk/Adobe Stock; back cover (dragonfly), Catmando/Adobe Stock; back flap (UP), Lisa M. Gerry; (CTR), © Franco Tempesta; (LO), Rebecca Drobis/National Geographic Image Collection; 2-3, Edson Vandeira/ National Geographic Image Collection; 3 (RT), Marcio Silva/Alamy Stock Photo; 3 (LE), paleontologist natural/Shutterstock; 4-5, Walter Myers/Stocktrek Images/Getty Images; 5, AuntSpray/ Shutterstock; 6 (RT), Sogom08/Alamy Stock Photo; 6 (LE), goro20/Adobe Stock; 7, Cory Richards/National Geographic Image Collection; 8-9, lapis2380/Adobe Stock; 8, Yuris C. Hassan/ Shutterstock; 9 (UP), Scenics/Alamy Stock Photo; 9 (LO), Wirestock/Adobe Stock; 13 (UP), Catmando/Adobe Stock; 16 (RT), © Franco Tempesta; 17, © Franco Tempesta; 23 (UP), © Franco Tempesta; 30 (UP), © Franco Tempesta; 30 (LO), ligasveta/Adobe Stock; 31 (UP), © Franco Tempesta

Library of Congress Cataloging-in-Publication Data

Names: Lisa M. Gerry, author.
Title: Big words for little paleontologists / Lisa M. Gerry.
Description: Washington, D.C. : National Geographic Kids, [2023] | Audience: Ages 4-8 | Audience: Grades K-1
Identifiers: LCCN 2022036920 (print) | LCCN 2022036921 (ebook) | ISBN 9781426375972 (hardcover) | ISBN 9781426376009 (library binding) | ISBN 9781426376412 (ebook)
Subjects: LCSH: Paleontology--Juvenile literature. | Paleontologists--Juvenile literature. | Dinosaurs--Names--Juvenile literature.
Classification: LCC QE714.5 .G39 2023 (print) | LCC QE714.5 (ebook) | DDC 560--dc23/ eng20230106
LC record available at https://lccn.loc.gov/2022036920
LC ebook record available at https://lccn.loc.gov/2022036921

Printed in China
23/LPC/1